The Gypsy's Revenge

A Comedy Melodrama

Michael Lambe

A Samuel French Acting Edition

SAMUELFRENCH-LONDON.CO.UK
SAMUELFRENCH.COM

Copyright © 1983 by Samuel French Ltd
All Rights Reserved

THE GYPSY'S REVENGE is fully protected under the copyright laws of the British Commonwealth, including Canada, the United States of America, and all other countries of the Copyright Union. All rights, including professional and amateur stage productions, recitation, lecturing, public reading, motion picture, radio broadcasting, television and the rights of translation into foreign languages are strictly reserved.

ISBN 978-0-573-11151-8

www.samuelfrench-london.co.uk

www.samuelfrench.com

FOR AMATEUR PRODUCTION ENQUIRIES

UNITED KINGDOM AND WORLD EXCLUDING NORTH AMERICA

plays@SamuelFrench-London.co.uk

020 7255 4302/01

Each title is subject to availability from Samuel French, depending upon country of performance.

CAUTION: Professional and amateur producers are hereby warned that *THE GYPSY'S REVENGE* is subject to a licensing fee. Publication of this play does not imply availability for performance. Both amateurs and professionals considering a production are strongly advised to apply to the appropriate agent before starting rehearsals, advertising, or booking a theatre. A licensing fee must be paid whether the title is presented for charity or gain and whether or not admission is charged.

The professional rights in this play are controlled by Samuel French Ltd, 52 Fitzroy Street, London, W1T 5JR.

No one shall make any changes in this title for the purpose of production. No part of this book may be reproduced, stored in a retrieval system, or transmitted in any form, by any means, now known or yet to be invented, including mechanical, electronic, photocopying, recording, videotaping, or otherwise, without the prior written permission of the publisher. No one shall upload this title, or part of this title, to any social media websites.

The right of Michael Lambe to be identified as author of this work has been asserted by him in accordance with Section 77 of the Copyright, Designs and Patents Act 1988

CHARACTERS

Hortense Mudd
Victoria Mudd
Edward Fawcett-Strangely
Bela, the gypsy
Xenia, his daughter
Jethro Meadowgrass
Joshua Mudd
Fanny Mudd, his wife
Mabel Fygg, a servant
Victoria's child prodigy

The action takes place in a wood, a cottage and a room at the Hall

Time—the Victorian era

ACT I

SCENE 1 The wood. An afternoon in late winter
SCENE 2 The Mudds' cottage. A day or two later
SCENE 3 The wood. The next night
SCENE 4 The Mudds' cottage. A day or so later

ACT II

SCENE 1 The Hall. Some nine months later
SCENE 2 The wood. Later that night
SCENE 3 The Mudds' cottage. The next morning
SCENE 4 The wood. Later that day
SCENE 5 The Mudds' cottage. Later that day
SCENE 6 The wood. The next day
SCENE 7 The Hall. Later that night

ACT III

SCENE 1 The Mudds' cottage. A week later
SCENE 2 The Hall. That evening
SCENE 3 The wood. That night
SCENE 4 The Mudds' cottage. Later that night
SCENE 5 The wood. Later that night

AUTHOR'S NOTE

Scenes should be suggested by simple cut-outs and key pieces of furniture. For instance, the Hall could have a free standing window, a plush armchair and a table. These can be cleared in seconds either by "period" stage hands or by the cast. The aim is to whisk props and furniture on and off with the minimum of fuss in full view of the audience.

If an extra set of curtains is available and is hung dividing the stage, then one scene can often be set while another is in progress. But curtains are not essential.

Music should accompany scene changes. I have indicated where music should be used, as it is vital to the atmosphere of the play. Rehearsal with the pianist is needed to avoid actors being "drowned" by the piano at a dress rehearsal. In any case, the pianist should attend early rehearsals to get the feel of the play and experiment with themes and improvization.

The producer may wish to insert entr'actes. I have also used "Madame Vera ffester" with good effect to sing *Rule Britannia* and *Land of Hope and Glory*, with audience participation! An entr'acte is also useful as an alternative to an interval, but if an interval is required the producer can place this where desired. Alternatively, the piece can be played, exhaustingly, straight through!

Lighting should be dramatic. For instance, a green spot should be used for Edward. The producer should explore the use of shadow and aim to light only the acting areas. A gauze would be useful for the ghosts but it isn't essential if their make-up is greyed. Otherwise, lighting, like the staging, is up to the resources and imagination of the company.

For Joan, Ray, James and Clive—
in memory of many melodramas

ACT I

Scene 1

A wood. An afternoon in late winter

The wood is a tree with a placard on it saying: "A Wood"

Hortense and Victoria Mudd enter. Hortense is the jolly daughter, Victoria, her tragic sister

Hortense Come along, Victoria, 'twill soon be dark and we still haven't gathered any wood. We must get some, or Father will beat us again, on our return to our poor hovel.
Victoria We may be lucky, Hortense; he may have died while we were away! Some good fortune must surely attend us afore long. The Lord, indeed, has smitten the family hard; what with Mother's consumption, Father's drinking, the mange that's stricken the goats; we do suffer so. I know not how we shall manage during the winter. Even the geese have impetigo. But no doubt it is all God's plan. Remember Job's boils!
Hortense I wish I had the learning like you, Victoria. It must be a wunnerful comfort. All I can do when I'm frettin' is to go to the privy, and torment the cat.
Victoria But you do have Jethro. At least you've a young man.
Hortense He's not much, but he's all there is, since the blight took the illegible. The village could do with some young bloods.
Victoria Indeed it could. My chance of matrimony is far off. And I so long to be a fine lady, with crisp linen sheets, a pillow of my own——
Hortense And a bed, Victoria. That would be nice. Save sleeping with the pig.
Victoria But such luxuries are not for the like of us. Come, Hortense, to our task.

They separate, to grub underneath the tree

Edward Fawcett-Strangley, the wicked young squire, enters

Villain's music

Edward The damned horse threw me and I've bruised my foot kicking the beast to death. What a bore. As is the country: full of odours, dung, and dreary peasants. I wish I had not had to leave London, but my father left me the estate only on the promise that I lived at Scratchings, the name of our country seat, for at least a year and a day. There is still a year to go, and the tedium appals. I rose at ten this morning and rode at twelve. I shot

things from one to two. Another ride and it is barely four. My God, I'm bored. But what have we here! Two young maidens if I'm not mistaken! Sport indeed! I shall approach them. (*Approaching*) Good-day, fair wenches. What do you in this drear forest?
Hortense (*curtsying*) Good-day, fine young sir, begging your pardon, like.
Victoria Why, sir, you limp. Are you afflicted?
Edward No, no. An old war wound, incurred when I was fighting the heathen. 'Tis nothing. But how considerate of you to ask. Pray, let me introduce myself. My name is Edward Fawcett-Strangely, the new squire of this parish.
Victoria Why, is the old squire dead?
Edward If he's not he'll be deuced uncomfortable. We buried him last week. And what are you both called?
Hortense I am Hortense Mudd, and this is my sister Victoria.
Edward Victoria Mudd; what euphony. How the name trips lightly off the tongue. Where do you live?
Hortense With our parents. Father was the squire's gamekeeper until he got the sack, and Mother boils underwear for the big house.
Edward Then I am your landlord! What a fortuitous meeting! (*Aside*) Fortuitous indeed! Perhaps we can arrange something better for your good parents.
Victoria Oh, sir, would you care to come home to our poor hovel? You could bathe your affliction.
Edward How beautifully you speak, Miss Victoria. But I fear I cannot walk far; the wound throbs, you know. Damn those Matabele. Excuse me, Miss Mudd. I forgot I was in the presence of the fair and genteel.
Victoria We cannot leave you here in this wood at dark. There are strange beasts at large.
Hortense Yes, indeed, Squire. We've had three ducks throttled this very week, and we know it wasn't Father. Some say it's the gypsies; some say it's the work of the devil.
Edward I am not afraid of gypsies, nor the powers of darkness.

An owl hoots and an animal screams

(*Cringing*) But if you would be so kind as to carry me to your wretched house. I see it is getting dark.
Hortense Come along, young Squire.

She hoists him on her back

Edward How very kind. And on the way I'll tell you of my life; my exploits in the Sudan where I conquered the mad Mogul, my famous balls——
Victoria Such excitements. I long to hear. Oh, how I would like to travel and see strange sights.
Edward Who knows, Miss Vicky, you may!

They all exit, Edward leering at the audience

The villain's music changes to a gypsy theme

Act I, Scene 1

Bela enters. He is a gypsy and a werewolf. He is followed by Xenia, his daughter, aged fifteen

Night deepens

Bela Come, daughter, deeper into this wood, away from prying eyes.
Xenia Soon the moon will be full, Father.
Bela Already my blood quickens. Accursed are we who bear the mark of the beast. Driven from village to village, forced to rend and tear the bodies of the innocent to satisfy the ancient bloodlust. Can we never find peace? Afore long, Xenia, you will join the pack; on the sixteenth anniversary of your conception you will become a werewolf.
Xenia I do not deny my ancient birthright, Father. But at times I am lonely; I long for a normal life—a home, little ones of my own playing around the hearth, gnawing their bones.
Bela Do not despair, daughter. Here we may find rest. The villagers know us not—and if we are careful we may rest here. But see—the moon!

The moon rises slowly. Bela stares transfixed and then begins to growl

The beast comes upon me! (*He howls and shrinks down*)

Bela lopes off, howling

Xenia Lords of the forest, gods of the glens, look down in pity on your child. Protect him through the night; keep him from harm, from the silver bullet fired in wrath or love. Let him not harm human kind for fear they should again seek us out, and drive us once more on the endless road of travail. I, Xenia, beg you to succour all werechildren while the moon be full. (*She sinks to her knees in supplication*)

Villain's music

Edward enters

Edward I lingered too long at the Mudds' and now am lost in this damned forest. But what have we here! A gypsy maid, praying to the moon. What sport! Victoria can wait awhile; here is more immediate enjoyment!
Xenia Lords of the great oaks, if it be your will, send me a sign of your favour.
Edward In answer to your prayer, I come, fair maid of the forest.
Xenia Oh, sir. Be you a man? Or a dryad?
Edward A man—as I shall surely shortly show. (*Aside*) Alliterative beast! To whom do you offer supplication?
Xenia To the great god, Pan, and his lordlings, to protect my poor father.

There is a howl, from afar

Edward It sounds as if he needs protection!
Xenia Oh no, sir, that be his hunting cry.
Edward (*aside*) Take care, Edward, lest you should stray out of your depth. What are you called, fair one?
Xenia Xenia, sir. My father is Bela, the gypsy. We are new to these parts.

Edward Then you shall come under my protection. I am your squire. Have you a tent or hovel in which you reside?
Xenia Only our caravan, sir. The wheel came off and shattered. We were looking for the wherewithal to mend it.
Edward The night grows colder. Come, let me escort you to your quaint dwelling. There we shall leave a note for your father.
Xenia Oh, sir, he cannot read.
Edward (*aside*) Even better. Then I shall take you to the Hall where you will find warmth and proper shelter!
Xenia You are so good to me, sir.
Edward And I'm sure you will be good to me in return. Come. (*Aside*) I'm much less bored now! (*He cackles*)

They exit R

The villain's music changes to Jethro's theme

Jethro Meadowgrass enters L. *He is betrothed to Hortense*

Jethro Hortense? Hortense? Where be the dratted girl. She said she'd gone wood-gathering with Victoria, and I thought I'd follow and give her a fright. Now I've gone and lost myself in this dratted wood in the dark.

There is a howl

And there's wolves around, unless it's the parson having one of his turns. The bosk is nowhere to spend the night alone.

An owl hoots

Oh dearie, dearie me. What a predicament. I think I hear her now, crashing through the bushes. That's cheered me up.

Bela, the werewolf, enters unseen by Jethro

I don't feel alone no longer. And I think I hear my Hortense.

The werewolf comes behind him

I can feel her breath—and smell it! (*He reaches behind him and feels its nose*) It's all wet! Have you got a cold, Hortense?

It snarls

Sounds like you've got a frog in your throat. Time you were in bed, tucked up warm. Come along, hold my hand. After all, I am your finance.

He exits holding the werewolf by the hand

There is a ferocious snarling and screaming, off

(*Off*) Why, Hortense, I never knew you were so passionate. Stop nibbling my neck or I'll have your ear off, you naughty flibber-me-gibbet.

There is a shriek and a howl, off

The werewolf lopes across the stage, looking fearfully back

Act I, Scene 2

Jethro enters in pursuit

Hortense, come back. I won't harm you. Come on, I can't see in the dark.

Jethro exits, pursuing the werewolf as——

the CURTAIN *falls*

SCENE 2

The Mudds' cottage. A day or two later

Mrs Mudd is boiling a vat of underclothes. She is a consumptive and coughs horribly throughout. We hear pig-squealing, off

Mrs Mudd Joshua, Joshua, do give over strangling that pig, I can't hear myself think. (*To herself*) I half wish new squire hadn't sent his underthings; I don't know how long you boil silk. Better add some more lye. (*She pours it in*)

Mr Mudd enters. He is the village drunk

Mr Mudd Give over coughing, Fanny. 'Tis honest work and he pays you well. 'Tis fortunate he's taken so to our Victoria.

Mrs Mudd 'Tis true, and yet I have my doubts about his intentions— (*peering into the vat*)—as well as his drawers. (*Pulling out a ragged pair of combinations, now in holes*) Oh dear, they've shrunk. You'd think he could afford better material.

Mr Mudd Well hurry up with the washing; the pig's gotter go in next if we want any dinner. And stop coughing.

Mrs Mudd It's me lungs. I fear I am not long for this world!

There is a knock at the door

Edward enters. He has claw marks on his cheek

Edward My dear Mrs Mudd, forgive my intrusion.

Mrs Mudd I do hope you haven't come for your washing, sir, it isn't quite ready. I must take the pudding out of your vest.

Edward (*aside*) Repellent rustic! No, indeed. I was passing by and I thought I would call on Victoria, with your permission, of course.

Mr Mudd She's mucking out the cow, sir. Shall I fetch her?

Edward If you would be so kind. And if we might have a moment or two together? This small coin may be some recompense for your bother. (*He tosses a coin to Mr Mudd*)

Mr Mudd Thank'ee, kind sir. Come, Mother, we'll send Victoria to Mr Edward and you can have a nice cough over the sheep.

Mr and Mrs Mudd exit

Edward Since that encounter the other night with the gypsy girl me loins are all aflame. A pity I had to dispose of her after I had had my way with her, but the slut talked of marriage and making her a lady. The fool, to think I would marry a trollop. I've left her body hanging in the woods. People will say she's a poor suicide, gypsies are always doing such things. And her father, whoever he is, has no idea of my identity. But I still yearn for pliant, warm flesh! My lusts know no bounds.

There is a knock at the door

Soft, what is that? My fair Victoria?

Bela enters

Bela 'Tis I, sir. Bela, the poor gypsy.
Edward Gypsy! (*Aside*) Quiet, beating heart!
Bela And who are you, noble sir?
Edward My name is—Joshua Mudd. This is my cottage. What do you want?
Bela I seek my daughter, sir. She did not return to our caravan the other night. I thought she might have wandered into the village. We are strangers in these parts.
Edward I regret I have not seen your daughter. Now be off with you. I have work to do.
Bela What are those marks on your cheek? They look like claw marks.
Edward Scratches, I wandered thoughtlessly into a hawthorn bush.
Bela I hope, for your sake, that it is all they are.
Edward Are you threatening me, Gypsy? Be off, or I'll set my dogs on you.
Bela They will not harm me, they are my friends.
Edward But the constabulary are not. Vacate these premises or I shall summon them.
Bela Very well, young sir, I'll not trouble you further. But beware!
Edward Beware what?
Bela Just—beware.

Bela exits

Edward (*wiping his brow*) A nasty moment, Edward. But I fooled the old charlatan. "Beware" indeed. Of what have I to be afeared?

Victoria enters, unseen by Edward, and puts her hands over his eyes

Help! I confess!
Victoria Confess to what, Edward, dearest?
Edward Oh, Victoria, 'tis you, I thought for a moment—'tis but my jest, Vicky. Have you missed me?
Victoria Oh, Edward, you know I have. Last night was the most wonderful of my life.
Edward Of course it was! And there will be more still glamorous nights.
Victoria To think that I shall be a fine lady, and live in London.
Edward Not for some months at least, Victoria. You know the condition my father imposed in his Will. Nor may I marry until then.

Act I, Scene 2

Victoria It will soon pass, Edward.
Edward Indeed, Victoria, in your arms the hours will fly like maddened moths.

They embrace

Come, let us retire to your warm bed of straw, and there dally awhile. Men have needs they must satisfy you know, or their hair falls out.
Victoria I know not of such things, Edward, but we cannot retire upstairs. Hortense is up there plucking the fowl, for to make a feather mattress.
Edward Then let us go for a walk, behind the cowshed. Come!

They encounter Mr and Mrs Mudd at the door

Mrs Mudd Excuse us, sir, we couldn't help overhearing. The keyhole is quite large.
Mr Mudd So you propose to marry our Victoria!
Edward Eventually, Mr Mudd. Victoria will explain the terms of my father's Will.
Mrs Mudd Those are indeed joyful tidings. Will you not stay for dinner, Squire? We can boil up the pig in a jiffy.
Edward Thank you, no, good lady. (*Aside*) Horrendous hag!
Mr Mudd Then come back to supper, Edward, and have a trotter or two.
Mrs Mudd And my belly will be cold by then.
Edward (*aside*) Vile creatures, will we never escape? (*To them*) Thank you for your kind gesture, but I have business to attend to this evening. Come, Victoria.

Edward and Victoria exit

Mr Mudd Such news, Mother. I'll away to the inn for some ale, and get you a new bottle of cough mixture. We must celebrate.
Mrs Mudd Yes, indeed. For once my lips shall touch the bottle. I am so excited. (*Calling*) Hortense, Hortense, leave your frettin' and hither here.

Hortense enters, with feathers

Hortense My, Mother, you be so flushed. You haven't been at Father's liniment, have you?
Mr Mudd Our Victoria is to be wed.
Mrs Mudd To Squire Edward! What do you think of that!
Hortense Knock me down with a mouldy polecat. She's a quick worker, she only met him the other day. Are you sure?
Mrs Mudd Edward told us himself. Mind you, the wedding cannot be immediate.
Hortense I knew there'd be a catch.
Mrs Mudd But that gives us plenty of time to prepare. Go, husband, and inform Parson.
Mr Mudd That shall I do, Mother.

Mr Mudd exits

Mrs Mudd And you, Hortense, look to your laurels with young Jethro and we can have a double ceremony before I'm in the grave. I always hoped, when I married your father, for better things. The Ponds were, after all, a genteel family, and did not wish me to marry beneath myself. I'll away to tell the neighbours. Such news!

Mrs Mudd exits

Hortense Who'd have believed it. Well I never. I can see I shall have to make an honest man of Jethro after all. He be not much to look at, but men are all the same in the dark

There is a knock at the door

Oh, that be he now. Come in, my wild geranium. Oh!

Bela enters

Bela Pardon my intrusion, good mistress, but who was that fine young gentleman who left with the young lady a short while ago?

Hortense You obviously don't mean Father, so it must be Mr Edward Strangely-Fawcett, the new squire.

Bela And the young woman?

Hortense That be our Victoria. She and Mr Edward are to be married—eventually. Why do you wish to know? Do you want to tell their fortune?

Bela If my suspicions are correct, indeed I do! Thank you, and farewell. (*Standing C and facing out front*) Horrible suspicions cross my mind! The scratches on his cheek. His evasiveness. If harm should have come to my Xenia, then revenge shall be mine and cursed retribution fall upon him and his dearest. I shall return to the woods to retrace her steps, and seek conclusive evidence. Beware, Edward, my fine fellow; your guilt will seek you out. As will the curse of the werewolf!

He exits to the sound of thunder and wild music

Hortense What a strange old man; I hope he bears no evil tidings. But what harm can befall us poor folk, that has not done already? And yet we survive, for we are British, and God has smiled upon this blessed isle set in the silvered, sceptred sea, our barrier against the feckless French and all foul foreigners. As long as the navy rules the oceans, and the Queen reigns supreme, little can trouble us. Other than the plague and ruin and unemployment and the weather and . . .

She exits, muttering as—

the CURTAIN *falls*

Scene 3

The wood. The next night

As before, the wood is represented by a tree with a placard. At the foot of the tree lies the body of Xenia. She has a rope round her neck and is clutching a handkerchief

There are owls and howls and then gypsy music

Bela enters

Bela I must be quick; the moon will soon be full. As yet no sign of Xenia, though I am sure she passed this way. Yes, see—footprints; one pair of bare feet and another of boots! She was accompanied—but by whom? Horrible suspicions cross my mind. (*Noticing Xenia's body beneath the tree*) What have we here? (*He drags out the body*) See, the blood. And rope around her neck. The clawmarks on the tree trunk! My child, my child! And in her cold claw—a kerchief. Initialled! Would I could read! But there be those that can; they shall confirm my darkest doubts.

The moon begins to rise

And even mourning is denied me, as the beast within awakes. Revenge! Revenge! (*He cradles her in his arms and howls piteously*)

The Lights fade and the music grows to a crescendo

Scene 4

The Mudds' cottage. A day or so later

Jethro I told 'ee afore, Hortense, I can't marry 'ee until I gets some money. I've nobbut tuppence ha'penny, and that won't pay for the honeymoon.
Hortense Perhaps Edward will give us some? He's got piles.
Jethro He shouldn't sit on wet grass.
Hortense No, silly, he's rich.
Jethro He's just sacked one pigman and a cowherd. Says he can't afford to pay them. Says he's hard up.
Hortense The agricultural recession truly affects us all, even those higher on the social ladder.
Jethro You do talk funny.
Hortense I am taking lessons from the parson. We must be couth if we are to be relations of Edward's.
Jethro Parson's daft, and so are you. Getting ideas above yourself. Know your place, my girl.

Hortense I'll have you know we come from gentle stock. My mother was a Pond!

Jethro Doesn't bother me if she was a puddle. We've all got a skeleton in the cupboard. (*He picks his nose*)

Hortense No, silly. Parson says we should combine Mother's maiden name with that of Father, it would sound better when banns are read; the union is announced of Edward Fawcett-Strangely and Victoria Pond-Mudd. Don't it sound genteel? Jethro, do stop picking your nose. You'll get worms.

Jethro I got 'em already, a few more won't make no matter.

Hortense If we are to marry, you'll have to learn to be a gentleman. I'm not having you show me up when we meet Edward's fine friends.

Jethro I'm not puttin' on no airs and graces, no, not for no-one. I'm plain stock and proud of it. The yeomen of England have been the backbone of this country for hundreds of years. We don't have fancy names like the gentry. Ours tell of honest toil; like Bull, Baker, Smith and Ploughright.

Hortense Yours is Meadowgrass.

Jethro And I'm proud of it. And I'm not having Parson reading out the union of Meadowgrass and Pond-Mudd!

Hortense Meadowgrass-Mudd's not much better.

Jethro It's what we're known by, Hortense, nothing to be ashamed of.

Hortense What was your mother's maiden name, Jethro?

Jethro Ducksfoot.

Hortense Oh dear. There must be some way to overcome the problem.

Jethro If I'm not good enough for you as I am, weddin's off. I bain't be goin' to change my ways.

Hortense And neither am I. I'd rather stay a maiden.

Jethro Maiden! That's a laugh.

Hortense Jethro Meadowgrass, what do you mean?

Jethro What about your carryin' on in the woods the other night. That weren't no maidenly behaviour.

Hortense I don't know what you mean!

Jethro All those love-bites you gave me in the dark.

Hortense I never did.

Jethro Course you did. Look here! (*He points to his neck*)

Hortense I was never in the woods. And I think you're carrying on with someone else. You ought to be ashamed. You've just come here to find an excuse to break off our engagement. For two pins I'd give you back your ring——

Jethro I never gave you one.

Hortense And that's another thing—you're mean. Go away, Jethro, you're spoiling everything. I'll never marry a man who thinks more of his cows than he does me. (*Weeping*) I'm going to be a fine lady like our Victoria.

Jethro She should know her station—and so should you. I'll not return until you come to your senses!

He stomps out

Mrs Mudd enters

Act I, Scene 4

Mrs Mudd Why be you a-wailing, Hortense? Dad's not home, is he?
Hortense Jethro and I have quarrelled. He doesn't want me to be a lady and talk proper.
Mrs Mudd Then you forget him, my dear. With all Edward's relations I'm sure someone better will be forthcoming. You might even marry a lord! Or an honourable. Oh, I so long to see you and Victoria safely wed. (*Coughing*) Then you won't get lung rot from lying on damp straw and inhaling your father's breath. Perhaps I could even visit you in Lon-don when you're settled in your fine house.
Hortense Of course you can, Mother dear. And have muffins and meringues for dinner, tea and breakfast.

Victoria enters

Victoria Mother dear, such news. Edward wants me to live with him at Scratchings, as his housekeeper, until we're married. He says he must not continue to visit here as it encourages gossip in the village, which is bad for his position as landlord. He hopes you will agree.
Mrs Mudd Well, I don't know that it's proper.

Edward enters

Edward Proper? Of course it's proper, Mrs Mudd. I seek to protect your daughter's reputation. Under my roof she can come to no harm. (*Aside*) Foolish girl. She will thrive and blossom in more genteel surroundings.
Victoria I can prepare better there for the wedding, Mother. I can learn to sew silks, and do fretwork and other ladylike occupations.
Hortense And I shall visit you every day, Vicky.
Edward That may not be altogether convenient. But no doubt we can make some suitable arrangements.
Victoria Oh, do give your consent, Mother.
Mrs Mudd Very well, Edward, if you think 'tis for the best, I'll not stand in her way. Come, Victoria, I'll help you pack.
Edward She'll need none of her things, dear Mrs M; we have ample up at the Hall. My sister left her gowns behind when she eloped to Bulgaria with the coachman. Come, Victoria, say adieu to your dependants.
Victoria Farewell, Mama. Farewell, Hortense.

They embrace. Hearts and Flowers music

I'm sure I'm doing the right thing.
Edward Of course you are. (*Aside*) She'll warm my bed and be useful around the house—without pay! Come, Victoria, to your new home, and a new and better life!

Edward and Victoria exit

Mrs Mudd and Hortense weep quietly, as Hearts and Flowers music changes to the gypsy theme

Bela enters holding an initialled handkerchief

Bela Forgive the intrusion, but I crave a boon.

Mrs Mudd Forgive our tears, old gypsy man; they are mingled joy and sorrow. My Victoria has just changed her station. She is gone to the Hall to act as Squire Edward's housekeeper. 'Tis joyous, and sad, as I'm sure you will know, if you are a father.
Bela Indeed, good dame. I have just lost my only daughter, under somewhat different circumstances.
Mrs Mudd Oh, sir, a mother's heart grieves for you.
Bela She left this kerchief behind. It bears signs I cannot read. Perhaps you could help me.
Mrs Mudd I can read some letters. Let me see.

He gives her the handkerchief

See, here are initials E.F.S. Why, they're Edward's. What a coincidence!
Bela Indeed, yes. Perhaps she found it lying in the woods. It is the squire's you say.
Mrs Mudd Indeed, yes. It is the fellow to those I wash for him. Such fine linen.
Bela I thank you for your courtesy, and leave you these charms. (*Handing them over*) They are protection against—wolves and creatures of the night. Wear them if you value your lives!

Bela exits

Hortense What a strange man. Look, Mother, this looks like silver. And what a funny shape.
Mrs Mudd It's the pentagram, sign of the beast. 'Tis said to protect the wearer against werewolves. Oh, Hortense, suddenly I feel the chill of the grave. I fear for our Victoria and I know not why. I have strange premonitions.
Hortense I know, but Dad still married you.
Mrs Mudd I feel I should mourn. (*She wails*)

Mr Mudd enters, drunk

Mr Mudd Cease that caterwauling, woman, you've stampeded the sheep.
Mrs Mudd Drunk again, Mudd?
Mr Mudd I've had a few, in honour of Victoria's levitation. Where is she?
Hortense Gone.
Mr Mudd Gone?
Mrs Mudd Gone!
Mr Mudd Gone where?
Mrs Mudd To Edward.
Mr Mudd Edward?
Hortense Edward!
Mr Mudd What for?
Mrs Mudd As his housekeeper, till they're wed.
Mr Mudd And she never said goodbye. Hard, hard is my daughter's heart. (*He weeps*)
Hortense Cheer up, Father. You've still got me. Jethro and I have parted. (*She weeps*)

Act I, Scene 4

Mr Mudd weeps harder

Mrs Mudd And I fear I am not long for this wicked world! (*She weeps*)
Mr Mudd Ah well, there's a silver lining in every cloud. I hope she'll visit us when she's a fine lady.
Mrs Mudd If she's spared. Oh, my poor child! I fear for your safety.

They all weep

CURTAIN

Suitably mournful music

ACT II

Scene 1

The Hall. Some nine months later

The Hall could be suggested by a free standing lattice window, a table and an armchair. Nine months later can be indicated by a placard brought on, announcing "Act II, nine months later"

Edward enters

Edward Victoria is becoming rather a bore. Not only is she great with child, she has affected ways above her class, and becomes exceedingly tedious. I tire of her—and long for London with its more stimulating pleasures. Only another month or so, and I can be free. In the meantime the new maidservant may afford some pleasure. But how to dispose of Victoria? 'Tis said the gypsies have returned. I thought I'd seen the last of them when I had them evicted. If she should meet with an accident, the blame could be put upon them! Several sheep have already died mysteriously, their throats torn out, as if by wolves. Perhaps? Perhaps?

Victoria enters. She is heavily pregnant

Victoria There you are, Edward. Please summon the doctor, dearest, I fear my time is near.

Edward Doctor? What do you want with the doctor. Go into the garden and whelp there.

Victoria Do not speak so harshly to me, Edward, even tho' it be in fun.

Edward Fun! When did I last have fun! You have not shared my bed this many a month. I am obliged to seek my pleasures elsewhere. There are those more receptive, you know.

Victoria Not the sheep again, Edward, you swore you'd forsake——

Edward Silence, woman! Your nagging torments my brain. Haven't I enough to worry about already? The estate is losing money through your extravagance.

Victoria I've only purchased a second hand bassinet in preparation for the birth. And we must wed immediately, Edward, the child cannot be born out of wedlock. You must make an honest woman of me. Think of the shame you would bring upon my parents. And I would die from the disgrace.

Edward (*aside*) If only you would.

Victoria Let me summon my mother and father. I'm sure they will know what is best. And my mother is not long for this world.

Act II, Scene 1   15

Edward I have forbidden them this house. You are better off without them. They seek only to bleed me dry, always begging for cast-offs and handouts. They are not of my—our—class, Victoria. If—when—I marry you, I do not wish to take unto myself your relations; they are lowly bred.
Victoria Then I will go to them to seek their aid. Nay, Edward, my mind is made up.
Edward If you leave this house you will not return here! It will sever our engagement.
Victoria Oh, Edward, you are so cruel to a defenceless woman.
Edward You want always your own way, you gormless slut. Well, in this you shall not succeed. I am away to the flocks, wolves or such are worrying them. I bid you good-night!

Edward exits

Victoria Oh, what is to become of me? I feel so helpless. Perhaps my maidservant, Mabel, can assist. I shall summon her. Mabel Fygg!

Mabel enters. She is the impertinent servant

Mabel You called, madam?
Victoria Mabel, I am determined to see my mother again. Will you assist me across the fields. I loathe to travel unaccompanied in my present delicate condition.
Mabel No!
Victoria Impertinent girl, what mean you?
Mabel Master says you are not to leave the house. I will not help you.
Victoria Ungrateful wretch—you will be sorry for this. I'll have you dismissed.
Mabel I don't think you will. Master would miss me!
Victoria You are too familiar!
Mabel That's what I tell the master, but it don't stop him.
Victoria Abandoned hussy. You shame yourself.
Mabel You're the one to talk. At least I've been careful.
Victoria Leave my sight.
Mabel Suits me.

She exits

Victoria Oh, Edward, faithless Edward. What am I to do? I shall see my mother and father. I shall make my way across the fields and through the woods and throw myself on their tender mercy. Edward, foul betrayer, farewell!

Stormy music

Victoria exits

Edward and Mabel enter

Villain's music

Edward Well done, Mabel. The plan succeeded admirably.

Mabel I always do my best to please, sir.
Edward And so you do, my little minx. Go, fetch my cloak.

Mabel exits

Victoria will make little speed through the woods. I shall soon overtake her. The night is dark, she will stumble and break her neck, or be attacked by some gypsy vagabond! Then I'll be rid of both of them. Farewell, Victoria!

Edward exits, laughing horribly

The music rises to a crescendo

CURTAIN

SCENE 2

The wood. Later that night

Bela enters

Bela The young gentleman thought he was rid of me when he sent the constables to drive us from the commonland. I can bide my time, let him damn himself further, until he suffers the torments that I endure, each time the full moon ascends the skies. I must live immortal until released by the silver bullet. He must die in agony and writhe et ernally in hell fire. (*Kneeling*) Oh ye lords of the night, succour the shade of my Xenia and let her be avenged, then do with me what you will. (*Rising*) But soft, a stranger comes. (*He hides behind the tree*)

Victoria enters

Victoria I fear I can go no further; my footsteps falter. The pains come more quickly now; I fear the child may be born here in this dark forest. (*Sinking to the ground*) May heaven protect me and my child so nearly born. (*She faints*)
Bela (*stepping forward*) Here, my child, drink this. (*Handing her a bottle*) 'Twill ease the pain. Soon your time will come. Fear not, I will aid you. Drink deep now. Take my cloak and spread it round you.
Victoria (*reviving*) I thank you, sir. I was frightened of the night and of the strange beasts of the forest.
Bela Nothing shall harm you. See, (*he howls*) I bid the children of the night to protect you.

Answering howls

You are safe with me. (*Raising his arms*) O ye winged ones of the night, ye that creep upon four legs, ye that slither, guard well this mother and her cub as if they be your own!

Act II, Scene 2

Answering howls and hoots

But by the pricking of my thumbs, something wicked this way comes! (*He retires behind the tree*)

Edward enters, wearing a cloak and hat, and carrying a silver headed walking stick. He carries a lantern in the upstage hand

Edward She must be near here; she can't have gone far. Damn this lantern for illuminating so little. See! Footprints! They lead to these trees. Perhaps she is in labour already. If so, she will put up little resistance; their carcasses will feed the wolves! (*Seeing Victoria*) So, Victoria. You thought to disobey me! I'll teach you manners ere you die! (*He raises his stick*)
Bela (*darting from behind the tree and seizing the stick*) Monster! Dare'st raise thy hands to the defenceless! Prepare to meet thy maker, child of Satan!

They grapple. Thunder, lightning, howling and wild music

Edward Desist, or I'll have the law on you, Gypsy! Take that! (*He strikes Bela with the stick*)

Bela falls to the ground

Take that! And that! (*Edward beats Bela round the head with the stick*) And now for the mother!

As he advances the Lights dim and hideous howling, grunting and flapping are heard. Luminous eyes are seen

Back, back vile creatures, beasts. (*Ducking*) My God, bats too. The very forest is alive! Get back, I say.

The music rises to a frenzy

He exits, flailing

Dawn slowly rises, ruddily to the accompaniment of suitable "dawn" music. A bird sings. We hear a baby crying

Curtain

Scene 3

The Mudds' cottage. The next morning

The Lights come up on Mrs Mudd at her vat and Hortense skinning a rabbit — or some other animal

Hortense Where do you want the guts put, Mother?
Mrs Mudd In the bucket, dear. I'll boil them presently for soup. Then you might go a-wood gatherin'. This fire is nearly out. (*Coughing*) Oh, my lungs.

Hortense Cheer up, Mother. Perhaps you will be called soon to your heavenly rest. But I do hate being so poor.
Mrs Mudd I know, my dear. But suffering is sent to try us—and it surely does. I'm only thankful I'm not long for this world of travail.
Hortense I can't think why our Victoria refuses to send us any money. She can't have changed so much since she went to live with Edward.
Mrs Mudd Edward says she refuses to see us. So that is that. Be grateful you've a roof over your head in such bitter weather.
Hortense Winter's early this year. It's going to be a hard time.
Mrs Mudd We've shelter, and a fire. And enough to eat that's wholesome— usually. So give thanks to Our Lord, and don't be so down in the mouth. I hates a mitherer. And hurry up with that animal—Father will be home soon and he'll want his supper.
Hortense I can't get the skin off; my fingers are numb.
Mrs Mudd Then use your teeth, my girl. That's what they're for.

There is a knock at the door

And see who that is

Hortense opens the door

> *Victoria staggers in with a shrouded baby in her arms. The child is huge and hairy, and should be played by a child of about eight*

Mrs Mudd Why, bless my soul, it's Victoria!
Victoria Mother, forgive me!
Hortense And she's got a babby with her!
Mrs Mudd Come and sit down, child, you look perished.
Victoria Oh, Mother, I have such dreadful news.
Mrs Mudd Hortense go and milk the goat. The child needs sustenance.
Hortense But I want to hear the bad news.
Mrs Mudd Get about your duty, my girl, or you'll not sit down for a week. There'll be plenty of bad news for all, I fear.

Hortense exits

Well, Victoria, what's to do?
Victoria Edward tried to kill me!
Mrs Mudd Lawks a land sakes, girl, do you know what you're saying?
Victoria I was coming home, Mother, when I was taken in labour. An old gypsy sheltered me while I gave birth. But Edward appeared out of the night like a monstrous demon. He made to kill me, but the gypsy struggled with him. Edward beat the gypsy wildly with his stick, and fled the forest. The old man, I fear, is dead. So I dragged my weary way home.
Mrs Mudd But why should Edward behave so ill to his child? So near to his marriage?
Victoria We will never be married, Mother. He wants to be rid of me. He says I am a clog unto his ambitions.

Hortense enters with the milk

Act II, Scene 3   19

Hortense Here's the milk, Victoria, warm and frothing from the goat. Perhaps if we dip the end of your cloak in it, the baby will suckle? I'll try my finger first to get it used to the taste.

She dips her finger in the milk and offers it to the child. There's a snap and she springs back

It nearly had my finger off. (*Peering closely*) Why, Victoria, it's got fangs! 'Tis unnatural!
Mrs Mudd Some babies are born with their teeth, Hortense. Don't be so daft. Try it with the cup, Hortense. See if it will swallow.

Hortense gives the child the cup and it spits out the milk

Well I never! Here, Hortense, fetch that old box; we'll put the little creature in that and try to settle it. What is it, Victoria, boy or little girl?
Victoria It's difficult to say. It's covered in hair.
Hortense 'Tis unnatural! (*She goes to fetch the crate*)
Mrs Mudd That girl's got dafter since she broke it off with Jethro. They do say those spurned in love go funny in the head.
Hortense (*dragging over the crate*) Here we are, Victoria. And I've brought a bit of old blanket too. It'll be warm in there — and I'll keep him in, nice and safe.
Victoria (*putting the child in the crate*) Bless you both; without you I know not what I would have done. (*She weeps*)
Mrs Mudd There, there rest now. You're home.

Mr Mudd enters, drunk

Mr Mudd Mother, I'm home. What's for supper? Why, it's our Victoria. Come slumming at last, have you? Come to gloat over our poverty?
Mrs Mudd Shut your row, you booby. Edward's turned her out. Her and her baby.
Mr Mudd Turned her out! Turned her out! But what about the wedding?
Mrs Mudd There'll be no wedding!
Mr Mudd Shame, shame, Victoria. You was brought up decent, and now you return home an abandoned woman with the bastard fruit of your womb to bring disgrace upon us.
Victoria Father, forgive me.
Mr Mudd I find it hard to forgive, Victoria. I have always lived an upright life——
Mrs Mudd Upright! You're flat on your back most of the time! Take no notice of him, Victoria. He's been down at the inn again, good for nothing sot.
Mr Mudd Blame not me, Fanny, for Victoria's misdeeds. I have not sported myself in the squire's bed.
Mrs Mudd Chance would be a fine thing. Though from what I hear of Edward he makes overtures to anything that's warm.
Mr Mudd Wash your mouth out, woman. Talk not of men's concerns. Victoria, I know not what will become of you. You cannot stay here.
Mrs Mudd You can't turn her out—she would die of cold. And there's the

child to consider. Regard your grandchild and your heart will soften.
Mr Mudd (*bending over the crate*) It's an ugly brute, Victoria. Here, pretty baby. (*He offers it his finger*)

It snaps

My God, Victoria, it's a wolf!
Victoria It is my child, Father. I shall not reject it, even though you spurn me.
Mr Mudd I am sorry I spoke harshly, my daughter. (*Proffering the rabbit*) Here, baby, play with this.

Sounds of chomping and a belch come from the crate. The child tosses out the rabbit skin

Well, did you ever see anything like it! Raw meat and it's—how old is it, Victoria?
Victoria But twelve hours!
Hortense 'Tis unnatural. Kill it, Father, before it does for us all!
Victoria Hortense, how can you be so wicked. I would die before I let you harm my baby. (*She springs to its defence*) Oh! (*She collapses*)
Mrs Mudd There now, see what you've done with your wild talk. Help her to the chair. Let's have no more of killing the baby. Victoria and her child are welcome here, so that's that. Oh, my lungs! (*She coughs and collapses*)
Mr Mudd That child's accursed! Mother, Mother can you hear me? Out cold. Go, Hortense, and fetch the doctor. Hurry, girl.
Hortense I'm sorry, Victoria, I'm sorry, Mother, for being so unnatural.

She exits

The baby cries. Sorrowful music

CURTAIN

SCENE 4

The wood. Later that day

Edward enters

Villain's music

Edward I was sure it was here that Victoria and the old gypsy met their deaths. But there is no sign of any body. Can I be mistaken? No, here are the signs of the struggle. Strange! I could even believe in the pathetic fallacy—that nature itself intervenes in our affairs—were I superstitious. Someone approaches. I must conceal myself. (*He hides behind the tree*)

Hortense runs on and stops, out of breath

(*Stepping out from behind the tree*) So, Miss Mudd. What do you here?

Act II, Scene 4   21

Hortense Edward! Is it true?
Edward Is what true, gormless girl?
Hortense That you tried to kill Victoria and her child?
Edward (*aside*) So they live! Curses. Certainly not. Victoria fled from my house in a temper, almost deranged. She drinks, you know. I had denied her access to the Madeira. I followed in case she came to harm, then was attacked by a mad gypsy. I fought with him to protect Victoria, and received a nasty blow on the head, which rendered me unconscious. When I came to, Victoria had disappeared. I am glad to learn that she is safe.
Hortense She is, Edward, but ill. She and Mother are both very poorly. I am on my way to fetch the doctor.
Edward A noble deed. But on my horse I can make better speed than you. I will summon the doctor for you. You go to my house and rest awhile. The servant will give you refreshment. It won't cost much.
Hortense Thank you, Edward. I am short of breath. But hasten, hasten.

She exits

Edward Hasten indeed. Not likely. Now, how can I conveniently dispose of Victoria? She's become a millstone round my neck and the child complicates matters. How can I ensure their speedy death? Set fire to the cottage secretly? Possibly, possibly. But soft, who approaches? 'Tis the old gypsy! I thought for sure he was dead! Perhaps I can turn this chance meeting to my profit. I say, old man, hither here a moment, will you?

Bela enters and approaches Edward

Look here, I'm sorry I was so rough with you last night. I thought you were a beast.
Bela I am.
Edward There you are, you see. Easy to make a mistake in the dark. Please accept this sov—this shilling and we'll say no more about it. (*He gives him a coin*) Does your head hurt much?
Bela There is no pain. I took a draught of my own preparation; it numbs the senses, instantly, and promotes a sound rest.
Edward Does it, by God! And if taken in too large a quantity?
Bela 'Twould cause a deep, deep sleep—and then death!
Edward Fascinating! Such a potion would be useful to me. I could use it on my bull. It gets very frisky at this time of year, and makes unwelcome advances to me when I enter its pen. How much for a large bottle?
Bela One piece of gold.
Edward Have you the substance at hand?
Bela I am never without it. (*He produces a large bottle marked with a skull and crossbones*)
Edward (*handing over the money*) I thank you, Gypsy. No doubt you will be moving on soon?
Bela Quite soon, I think.
Edward Good, good. (*Aside*) Don't want any witnesses!
Bela Tonight the moon is full!
Edward How quaint. Never bothered with it much myself.

Bela Beware, young sir, beware!

Bela exits

Edward Strange old cove. Must have a head like a rock. Enough of him. I shall haste to Victoria, in the guise of a doctor, and administer the draught. You shall surely sleep the peace of the just tonight, Victoria. You and your brat!

Edward exits, cackling horribly

Bela enters

Bela Had he not beaten me with that stick of silver head, I would have killed him already. Now he goes to murder his wife and child, and can be apprehended by the very law he used against me. There is justice indeed! However, I shall watch with care. Should there be error, Edward will still face the vengeance of the werewolf! Tonight the moon is full!

Bela exits cackling

Wild gypsy music

CURTAIN

SCENE 5

The Mudds' cottage. Later that day

Hearts and Flowers music

Mrs Mudd and Victoria are slumped in chairs and Mr Mudd is in attendance. The child is in the crate

Mr Mudd (*attentively*) Where be that doctor? I fear he will be too late. Oh, my Fanny. I have wronged you vilely. Speak, speak to us, Fanny.

Mrs Mudd I fear I am not long for this world, Father. Swear you will safeguard Victoria and the little one.

Mr Mudd Your words have touched me, Fanny. I swear I will forsake the demon rum. I am a changed man.

There is a cry from the crate

Does the little one need feeding again? It's not an hour since he had that rabbit!

Mrs Mudd He has a healthy appetite! But there is no more food, alas. Give him your thumb to suck.

Mr Mudd (*giving his thumb to the child*) Gladly, my Fanny. (*He screams in pain*) He's chewed it to the bone! (*Snatching his hand away*) Look, Fanny, look!

Child (*showing his hairy face and hands over the crate*) More, more.

Act II, Scene 5   23

Mrs Mudd Why, it can speak! 'Tis a miracle.
Mr Mudd 'Tis unnatural!
Child Mother, Mother!
Victoria (*stirring*) What is it, little one?
Mr Mudd Have it put down, Victoria.
Child No, no, dearest grandpapa. Fear not; I am but a prodigy. But, Mother, I fear I am not long for this wicked world.
Mr Mudd It runs in the family!
Child I have a strange premonition.
Mrs Mudd I expect we'll get used to it.
Victoria What premonition, little one?
Child That I am to be foully slain by the hand of one that should be dear to me! And you, Mother, beware! Beware!

There is a knock at the door

Edward enters in a false beard and cloak

Edward Dr Drummitt at your service. Where are the afflicted?
Mrs Mudd Well, there's me. I'm not long for this world, Doctor. And our Victoria here; she's very poorly. And the child's not up to much. Neither is my husband really, begging your pardon like.
Edward Dear me, is it the plague?
Mrs Mudd No — more like rheumatism in the chest, if you'll beg my pardon for attempting a diagnosis, not being properly qualified like ...
Edward Say: "ah".

She does so

My God, woman. I've never seen anything like it. What's that strange growth in your mouth?
Mrs Mudd (*inaudibly*) My 'ong.
Edward The nastiest 'ong I've ever seen. You are truly sick, madam. And where are the other patients?
Victoria I am one, sir.
Edward You look pale and loitering. Do you sweat?
Victoria I perspire a little.
Edward Do you have to use the privy?
Victoria Most days.
Edward Say "Mulier hominum confusio est".
Victoria I can't manage that, sir.
Edward Premature softening of the brain! You are indeed unwell.
Victoria And my little one is horribly afflicted.

There is a coughing noise from the crate

Hark!
Edward Indeed, yes. A nasty case of the staggers — probably caught from mare's milk. Have you been feeding it yourself? No matter. Fortunately I have a cure, a specific for all these complaints. (*To Mr Mudd*) If you, sir, would care to hand over one guinea, your family shall be cured.

Mr Mudd A guinea! That's a fortune.
Edward This drug does not come cheap; neither does my time!
Mr Mudd We've nobbut three shillings in our savings.
Mrs Mudd And that's for Hortense's trousseau. Think not of me, Mudd. I am not long——
Mr Mudd Take two shillings, Doctor. Otherwise I shall have to call in the apothecary—he's cheap.
Edward Your words have touched my heart, Mr Mudd. I am not on this world for profit, nor would I disgrace my hypocritic oath. Here, take the nostrum with my compliments! (*Handing over the bottle*) About one third of the bottle to each patient should do it. And so, farewell, I must away to de-louse the vicar

Edward exits, bowing

Bela's face appears at the window

Stormy music mounts during the following

Mr Mudd Right then, Mother. You be first. No need to dirty spoons. Just take a swig.

She does so. He takes the bottle back

And now the babby. Here little one. Here's your nice medicine!
Child (*peering from the crate*) No, no I fear the worst!
Victoria Come, Father, give me the bottle. The child is afraid of your rough ways. Here you are, dearest. Take it to please Mama.
Child Very well, Mother. I am obedient to your wishes. Farewell, wicked world. (*Drinking the bottle dry*) See, Mother, I have spared you the fate you too would have suffered. Argh! (*He goes into prolonged convulsions and dies*)
Mr Mudd What ails it?
Victoria 'Tis dead! (*She swoons*)
Mr Mudd Mother—be you all right?
Mrs Mudd Fine, Father. I have this lovely warm glow in my—Argh! (*She collapses*)
Mr Mudd (*taking Mrs Mudd in his arms*) Mother, Mother, speak to me!
Mrs Mudd I am dying, Joshua. I hear the beat of angels' wings. Soon I shall join the feathered choir.
Mr Mudd Oh woe, woe.
Mrs Mudd Farewell, Joshua. (*She dies—almost*)

Mr Mudd bends down to kiss her

(*Rearing up*) Farewell! (*She dies*)

Mr Mudd mourns to sad music

CURTAIN

Act II, Scene 6

SCENE 6

The wood. The next day

Funereal music. Bela is hidden behind the tree

Jethro enters, wearing a black smock and carrying a shovel

Jethro Life certainly bain't be much fun of late. What with Mrs Mudd being called to her rest so sudden like, and the vicar refusing to bury the baby in hallowed ground, 'cos it weren't watered proper, and Mr Mudd going deranged—it don't make for 'appiness.

Hortense enters, wearing a black apron

Hortense Oh, there you are, Jethro. Is this the place?
Jethro The child left a note asking to be buried near the tree with the claw marks. Strange goings-on, if you ask me. Where be Victoria?
Hortense She's coming presently, with the baby. She had to chain Father up first. Poor man, he's quite demented. He bit the vicar, you know.
Jethro Madmen have fearful strength, so I'm reliably informed.
Hortense I'm so grateful to you for your help, Jethro. Can you ever forgive me for being so stupid?
Jethro No!
Hortense Oh, Jethro.
Jethro Come on, girl. I was only fooling. Once all this mourning and such like is over, we'll get married and raise pigs.
Hortense Oh, Jethro. I know it is the wrong time to feel happiness but you have moved my heart strangely. Bless you, Jethro, I will try to be a good wife. Lawks, who's that?

Bela steps from behind the tree

Bela 'Tis only I, mistress. Have no fear. I came to mourn the passing of the little one.
Jethro Ay, 'tis a sad business.
Bela Sadder than you know!
Hortense What do you mean?
Bela Stay—here comes the mother with the body!

Funereal music again!

Victoria enters, carrying the corpse of the child

Victoria Hush, little one. Not long now until you rest for ever in the peaceful earth. But it was hard to deny you a blessed plot. Bless you, Hortense, and you, Jethro—and you, good sir, for your presence. Come, let us prepare the grave.
Bela Wait, I beg of you. I crave a boon.
Jethro Hardly the time, good Gypsy.

Bela Never more opportune. Listen. I know how your mother and this prodigy came to their untimely deaths.
Hortense The doctor said 'twas apoplexy. There's a lot of it about.
Bela 'Twas no natural death!
Victoria What are you telling us, good sir?
Bela Give me the child's body to bury according to ancient rites and I will reveal all to you.
Victoria Never. My child shall rest here!
Bela Your child will never rest here.
Hortense What do you mean?
Bela 'Twas a prodigy. It could speak and make letters, could it not?
Victoria 'Twas well advanced for its age.
Bela Think of its father!
Jethro What do you mean?
Bela Its father seduced, then murdered, my daughter Xenia; fairest flower of our tribe.
Victoria What horrors you utter.
Bela Before she died, she bit him.
Jethro She would!
Bela Xenia was not wholly human. She bore the sign of the pentagram.
Hortense The mark of the beast!
Bela Precisely.
Jethro Then you must be——
Bela A werewolf. I too suffer the ancient curse. And you must know that whoever is bitten by a werewolf inherits the affliction.
Victoria Then Edward——
Bela Has inherited the strain, and passed it to his child.
Victoria But Edward showed no signs of the affliction.
Bela He would not. Xenia was but a maiden. In the gentler sex the transformation is delayed until maturity. But the male gard du loup shows himself at birth—if the moon be full.
Jethro Then the little one was a werewolf!
Bela Is a werewolf!
Hortense What do you mean?
Bela A werewolf can be brought to its eternal rest only by a silver bullet, through its heart, or by having its head removed with a silver knife.
Victoria You can't mean to mutilate my child!
Bela If it is not done the child will awake in the worm-ridden earth when the moon is full. He will claw his way out of his tomb, and wander through the forest, a ravening beast.
Victoria How horrible!
Bela My way will release his soul to wing its way to its heavenly rest.
Jethro 'Tis for the best, Victoria.
Victoria I suppose so. But it seems so cruel. Perhaps in a day or so——
Bela There is no time. Tonight the moon is full.
Victoria Very well, I will do as you ask. But I cannot stay to see the deed. Farewell, little one.

She exits, sobbing

Act II, Scene 7

Jethro Go with her, Hortense. 'Tis no place for you. This is man's work.
Hortense What do you mean?
Jethro Cease asking questions, wife to be. Go and assist Victoria.
Hortense Very well, Jethro. Oh, such sad times.

She exits

Jethro Well, Gypsy, what do you want me to do?
Bela Go gather wood for the funeral pyre. The body is best consumed by cleansing flames. I will stand guard and begin the rites.

Jethro exits

(*Standing over the body*) Peace, little one. Soon you journey through the vale of night, free from the curse of the pentagram. But you shall be avenged! I shall set Victoria's father free at Edward's door; a madman should dispose of Edward quite effectively. If not, another murder may be accredited to him, thus further securing his damnation, both by earthly and heavenly law. I will surely lead him to perdition and ensure he suffers the tortures I have suffered this long life. Look down, Xenia, from your home in heaven. Receive this child as one of our kind released from its earthy prison, and guide your father to his just revenge!

The Lights change to a red sunset, with Bela in sharp relief as——

the CURTAIN *falls to solemn music*

SCENE 7

The Hall. Later that night

A lighted candle stands on the table and through the window the moonlight shines fitfully through the clouds

Edward enters in a long dressing-gown. There is a howl outside and thunder

Edward What a fearful night! I have strange forebodings! Perhaps Mabel will afford me comfort—though her unsophisticated ways become tiresome. Even the goat is more inventive. Still, the night is cold. I shall summon her. Mabel! I must buy a bell.

Mabel enters with a tray containing two tumblers of drink

Mabel You called, me lord?
Edward Less of your sarcasm, me gel. Tho' you may indeed be speaking truer than you think. A knighthood is not beyond my means. And who knows what may follow that? Sir Edward? Lord Edward? Earl Edward—King Ed—perhaps too far. My ambition tends to vault above itself. But here I cannot make the right connections. I must away to London.
Mabel What are you going on about? Called me out of my nice warm room just to listen to you mumble to yourself? Must think I'm daft.

There is a howl and thunder

Lawks, just listen to that row. Not a night for christian folk to go a-stirring themselves. I've brought you a hot toddy—not that you deserve it. You neglect me something rotten.

Edward (*starting out of his reverie*) What? Oh, thank you, Mabel. Most considerate. (*Sitting in the armchair*) Light the fire will you?

Mabel There's no wood. I told you yesterday we were out. I also told you not to sack the other servants. I can't do it all you know. You make enough work without me having to hew wood.

Edward I have no need of more staff, Mabel. Soon I shall dispose of this mausoleum and return to London.

Mabel And where does that leave me, pray?

Edward What do you mean? Leave you? Here I should think. You'll be provided for. (*Aside*) A penny a week should suffice!

Mabel Oh no, Edward, you're not buying me off so lightly. I'm coming to London with you.

Edward Oh no you're not.

Mabel Oh yes I am!

Edward (*rising*) Do you think I would be accompanied by a third-rate, half-witted cretin, a drab such as you? What would my friends think!

Mabel So, I'm not good enough for you, is that it?

Edward You amused me—once. Now I find you tiresome.

Mabel Tiresome! I'll give you tiresome!

She throws her drink in his face and he strikes her to the ground

Edward Desist, you slut, or you shall join your Maker sooner than you intended!

Mabel (*rising*) I'm not frightened of you! (*She attacks him*)

They struggle. Edward retreats before her blows. She kicks him hard in the behind

Edward (*turning in fury and strangling her*) Die! Die! You whore!

Thunder and lightning as Mabel slumps to the ground

Feeble-minded cow. Now, how to dispose of the body?

There is a loud howl

My God, what was that?

The face of Mr Mudd appears at the window

Lightning and thunder

What a fearful apparition! Surely sent from hell to take my soul after this foul deed. I repent! I repent!

Mr Mudd bursts in, deranged, clutching a dagger

Mr Mudd Monster! Murderer! Violater! Prepare to meet thy infernal master! (*He rushes forward to strike*)

Act II, Scene 7   29

Edward (*dodging Mr Mudd*) Mr Mudd, have you taken leave of your senses!
Mr Mudd You did for my Fanny! (*He lunges at Edward*)
Edward (*circling*) I assure you I never touched her. Calm yourself!
Mr Mudd And the little one! Ah! See! The fiend comes for you!

Bela, as a werewolf, appears at the window

Edward Good Lord, what next? Desist, Mudd!

They fight fiercely. Mr Mudd runs on to his own dagger and sinks to the floor with a groan

Mr Mudd Fanny, forgive me! (*He dies*)
Edward Spared once more. Fortuitously, as it happens. The constable will believe that Mudd, in his madness, broke in here and strangled poor Mabel. I, hearing the commotion, rushed in and tried to save her. Mudd died on his own dagger. (*To Bela outside the window*) And as for you, be off or I'll set the law on you. I fear nothing; I am innocent. Innocent! (*He cackles*)
Bela (*from outside the window*) No, doomed, doomed! (*He howls*) Doomed to eternal damnation!

Loud thunder, lightning and wild music

CURTAIN

ACT III

Scene 1

The Mudds' cottage. A week later

Hearts and Flowers music

Victoria Woe, woe is me. My father slain by Edward, and the villain exonerated. Is there no justice to be found in this land? Are the rich forever to exploit the lowly? Yet I shall be avenged. Heaven will surely guide me.

Hortense and Jethro enter

Jethro Talking to yourself again, Victoria. 'Twill never do. You'll end up in the looney house.
Victoria I was imploring Heaven's aid in wreaking judgement on that foul villain Edward.
Hortense I doubt if the good Lord has time to listen to the likes of us, Victoria. He must be busy with more important things. At least that's what Parson said when I asked him why Mother was called so prematurely to her heavenly rest.
Jethro We poor, simple folk have to do the best we can: like catching Edward in the dark—on his own—with a pitchfork.
Victoria Surely his guilt must weigh hard upon his soul! Perhaps if I confronted him he would confess. No man can be so callous and hardhearted. Surely he fears Heaven's wrath?
Jethro He'll buy his way in, Victoria; he'll find some way to take his money with him.
Hortense Cheer up, Victoria. We're not so badly off. We've a roof over our heads, and a cow.
Jethro And there's two sheep left after paying for the funerals.
Hortense And we've still got the silver charms the gypsy gave us—they might fetch a bit. And Jethro's saved four whole shillings! I know it's hardly the time to mention it, Victoria, but Jethro and me were thinking of getting wed. We've not had a chance to say much about it, what with all the funeral arrangements. But I'm sure Mother and Father wouldn't mind. If we did it soon we could use the left-overs from Father's do, before they go off. There's half a ham over, and the weather's too cold for maggots.
Jethro The black pudden's lookin' a bit green.
Victoria Of course you shall marry. My blessing on both of you.
Hortense And do you mind if Jethro moves in here, till we're wed proper? Edward's selling the estate . . .
Jethro And anyhow, it didn't seem proper to go on working for him. I'll sleep with the cow.

Act III, Scene 1   31

Hortense No you won't!
Jethro I didn't mean you. Though, I don't know ...
Victoria I'm sure all will be for the best. I, of all women, am in no position to cast stones—nor would I wish to do so. Take my sister with my blessing, Jethro.
Jethro Where?
Hortense Do give over, you great fool, or I shan't marry thee.
Jethro Very well, Hortense Mudd, I take thee to be my awful wedded wife according to God's holy ordinance. Whatever that may mean. And I hitherto plot thee my trith. Here, you can have this ring from the old bull's nose.
Hortense And I plot my trith too, Jethro, dear.
Jethro Do we have our nuptils now, then?
Hortense We certainly do not. There'll be a bolster 'atween us until after the parson's said 'is bit. Come on, let's arrange the room.
Jethro It be like driving a coach a' four with the brakes on.

Jethro and Hortense exit

Victoria Some happiness, at least, there is upon this direly afflicted family. But at what cost? My mother and father dead, and my little one murdered by the same bloody hand. I will be avenged! I shall confront Edward with his misdeeds and trust in Heaven to protect me. At worst I shall be quickly deprived of my earthly bonds, and re-united with my loved ones. So, Edward, do your worst. Nothing can harm the righteous. Beware, Edward, your black deeds shall be exposed to the pure light of justice! Justice! Justice!

CURTAIN

"*Justice*" *music*

SCENE 2

The Hall. That evening

Edward stands drinking heavily—a roll of thunder!

Edward I must leave this place! I grow to fear the night. I dread the apparitions that haunt my soul and deny me rest. Nightly they come as the clock strikes eight.

A clock starts to chime and Edward counts with each chime

One! Two! Three! Four! Five! Six! Seven! Only seven o'clock. Thank God.

There is another chime

Ah! (*Staggering to his chair and slumping into it*) Horrors! The fearful fiends do come!

The ghost of Xenia appears

Xenia Look on my face, Edward. See where maggots fill the sockets where once my eyes shone forth. I await you, Edward.

She vanishes

The ghost of Mabel appears

Mabel Edward, Edward, confess your sins or writhe forever in the torment of the damned as do I. Fear the flames of hell, Edward! Your throne awaits you here.

She fades

The ghost of Mr Mudd appears

Mr Mudd O vile betrayer, seducer, villain. Forgiveness never can be thine. You shall roast in hell for eternity.

He vanishes

Mrs Mudd appears

Mrs Mudd My cough's quite gone, Edward. It's lovely here. Quite a rest really. But alas, Edward, 'tis not for you. Your destination lies below, amidst the ice-cold fires and molten seas. Satan himself will come for you. Farewell, Edward.

The ghosts of Xenia, Mabel and Mr Mudd join Mrs Mudd

Ghosts (*wailing together*) Farewell!

Thunder

The ghosts disappear

Edward Oh, what vile dreams. Yet dreams they are! Courage, Edward, believe not in them. Satan will come for you indeed! What rubbish!

There is a knock at the door. Edward screams and hides behind the armchair

Victoria enters

Victoria Edward? Edward, where are you? (*She looks round the room*)

He sneaks out from behind the armchair

Oh! Edward, you frightened me!

Edward Come to gloat, have you, miserable slut?

Victoria Not to gloat, Edward, never that. I came for justice!

Edward Justice! What know you of justice! That clearly is reserved for me!

Victoria What do you mean?

Edward Nightly the visions of your wretched father and mother appear to me. They haunt the house. Where e'er I go I seem to see them. Mocking me.

Victoria Pray, Edward, 'tis not too late. Pray for the forgiveness of Heaven and the mercy of those you have so wronged. Come, Edward, join me in prayer now.

Act III, Scene 2   33

Edward I'll try anything once—that's been my downfall!

They kneel. Pious music

Victoria Dear Lord, protector of the weak, look down upon your child, Edward, who now repents his foul deeds. Forgive him, Lord, he suffers much.
Edward Forgive me, Lord.

There is a crash of thunder and lightning

The ghost of the child appears

Child Think not Heaven heeds you, Edward. You are doomed!

The ghosts of Xenia, Mabel, Mr Mudd and Mrs Mudd appear

Ghosts (*together*) Doomed!
Edward (*rising*) Then damn the lot of you to hell's fires.

The ghosts vanish

I am not the man to cower. Heaven do your worst. I put my faith in hell.

Thunder and lightning

Bela's face appears at the window

Victoria (*rising*) Edward, do not blaspheme. I fear for your soul!
Edward Fear for your own, half-witted slut. Come, join your parents! (*He seizes her round the neck and throttles her*)

The ghosts appear and look on in a tableau of horror

Now, God, do your worst!

Thunder and lightning

Victoria I am dying, Edward.
Edward Well hurry up, then.
Victoria Heaven's vengeance will strike you down, Edward.

He kicks her

Oh, I die. (*She dies*)
Edward Free, at last! I'll bury the body in the woods. No-one will suspect me. Then to dispose of this place and away to London, ghosts or no ghosts. They can come if they wish. I fear no deathly spirits. My crimes are such, that all that is left, is to live life to the full, to drain its dregs, and then to seek the protection of the devil.

Bela howls outside

Come, Victoria, away to your final place of rest!

He starts to drag the body off to wild music, thunder and lightning

CURTAIN

Scene 3

The wood. That night

Eerie music

The grave is ready and Edward stands by the mound of earth holding a spade. Victoria's body is to one side of the stage. There is a full moon

Edward Even nature assists me in my deed. The moon affords ample light. The grave is dug and awaits only its occupant. I shall fetch her.

The moon disappears creating a Black-out

Curses. No lantern. Still, she's can't be far. She's not going anywhere.

During the Black-out, Bela, as a werewolf, gets into the grave or hides behind the mound (whichever is easier)

Full moonlight returns

(*Dragging Victoria's body towards the grave*) Come along, Victoria, do not dally. The worms await your once fair flesh! What's that round your neck? A silver charm? You won't be needing that! (*He removes the necklace and kneels*) A final prayer, Victoria? (*He laughs horribly*)

Bela springs out of the grave and grabs Edward by the throat

(*Rising and staggering backwards*) You!
Bela I, Edward. Bela the wolfman. Now is my vengeance complete. You die tonight.
Edward Not by your hand—or claw—I don't! (*He lashes out at Bela*)

They struggle and wild music plays as they fight. Edward strangles Bela with the silver charm necklace. In his agony, Bela bites Edward

Bite me, you cur. Then join the slut who already lingers here!

There is thunder and lightning as Edward topples the bodies into the grave

Lie there forever in rotting embrace. What's this? I bleed! Curse the old dog. Still, he's no more. I fear not the curse of the wolfman any more than his gibbering daughter. Murder is so very simple. I grow to like it. (*He snarls*) There's still the fair Hortense at large! My blood seems to thicken and strange forces stir within me! (*He howls*) Dear God, the mark of the beast!

He lopes off, contortedly to wild music

CURTAIN

Scene 4

The Mudds' cottage. Later that night
Thunder and lightning
Hortense enters in a nightgown

Hortense Jethro, Jethro, come downstairs. I'm afeared.

Jethro enters

These are portents, Jethro. Heaven is surely angry.
Jethro Not as angry as I be, you daft grummet, awaking me up for nothing! What have you come down here for? 'Tis chilly round me parts.
Hortense Give over complaining. I'm worried about our Victoria. She's not come home. I fear for her safety.
Jethro She'll be all right. She'll be spending the night up at the Hall. Perhaps she and Edward have become reconciled.

The ghost of Victoria appears

Victoria Not so, not so. Pity the dead, called untimely to their rest.
Hortense Heavens, it's our Vicky.
Jethro So it be! Be you properly dead, Victoria? It's all very sudden.
Victoria I cannot stay long. List. Make from your silver charm a bullet and fire it into Edward's body. That will destroy him, for he now bears the mark of the beast and is as monstrous in visage as he is in soul. Farewell. My blessing on you both!

Victoria fades away

Hortense Well, did you ever, whatever next? It's all too much for me. Vicky dead, yet not so. Whatever shall we do, Jethro?
Jethro Better do as she says, I suppose. If Edward is a werewolf, no-one will blame us for shooting him. I wonder how you make a silver bullet?
Hortense 'Tis easy. Take this (*she gives him the charm*) and melt it down over the fire, then pour it into the mould Father used to make his bullets in. Everyone round here knows how.
Jethro But we haven't got a gun.
Hortense Yes, we have. Father's. It's somewhere upstairs. He used to shoot cows with it when he was feeling bad.
Jethro Right, Hortense. To work! (*He prepares to hammer the charm*)

"Anvil" music

Hortense exits

CURTAIN

Scene 5

The wood. Later that night

Thunder and werewolf music

Edward enters. He is hairy and snarls

Edward Accursed! Accursed! Doomed forever to wander at full moon, seeking flesh to rend and blood to drink! Should I move to London, people will surely notice! Perhaps not! But doomed are my chances of the gay life—except at costume balls! But what is this? People coming? An early breakfast! I shall retire. (*He goes behind the tree*)

Jethro and Hortense enter. Jethro holds a lantern and Hortense has the gun concealed

Jethro You must be daft bringing me out here to track down Edward. It's his wood—he'll know every tree.
Hortense See, Jethro, tracks. Bring the light lower.

They examine the tracks. Edward stalks them

Jethro Never seen tracks like that before. Too big for a proper wolf!
Hortense They're Edward's, I'm sure of it!
Edward So right you are, interfering vixen. Prepare to die!
Hortense (*running*) Quick, Jethro, the gun!
Edward (*laughing*) Gun. I fear no guns. I am immortal!
Jethro You've got it. I gave it you. (*He runs after Hortense*)
Hortense No I haven't!
Jethro Yes, you have!

They run in a circle with Edward pursuing

It's in your drawers! You put it there for safe-keeping. Oh!

Edward grabs him

Hortense (*getting the gun*) Hang on, Jethro, I'll save you. Now, how do you work this thing?

Edward sees what she's doing, leaves Jethro and slowly stalks her

Edward Come, Hortense, bare your throat. I feel thirsty!
Hortense Drat this trigger. Oh!

Edward seizes her. She stamps on his foot then hits him over the head with the butt and he hops around howling

Take that from me and Victoria!

Jethro seizes the gun from her and fires. Edward howls hideously and sinks to the ground

Act III, Scene 5

Edward The bullet. The silver bullet. It gnaws my very vitals. Oh, the pain!

The ghosts of Xenia, Mrs Mudd, Mr Mudd, the child, Bela and Victoria gather in a hideous tableau to receive Edward

Edward points to the ghosts while Jethro and Hortense cower respectfully

Look! My welcomers await. Too late now for forgiveness. Farewell, wicked world.

He dies screaming as the ghosts bear his body away

Hortense Oh, Jethro. What strange sights we have beheld.
Jethro Life has certainly not been without incident.
Hortense Why, Jethro, you're speaking properly!
Jethro It must be catching. (*He starts to gyrate*)
Hortense What be the matter?
Jethro I dunno. I feel all—peculiar. Oh Lord, I remember.
Hortense Remember what?
Jethro The old gypsy—the other wolfman.
Hortense What of him?
Jethro He nibbled my neck in the woods—remember, I thought it was you.
Hortense But that was ages ago—and you've never manifested signs nor portents.
Jethro (*writhing*) I think I'm about to! (*He sinks down and starts to snarl*) It must be a delayed reaction. Schoolmaster always said I was a bit slow.
Hortense (*seizing him in an embrace*) You're not getting out of marrying me so easily. If you're going to be a wolfman then I'll be a wolfwoman——
Jethro Think of the cubs. What'll people say?
Hortense We'll just blame the gypsy's curse. Come on!

She drags him off as——

the CURTAIN *falls*

The CURTAIN *rises to reveal a tableau of the whole company or a grand parade of the characters, ending with Victoria and Edward, to the accompaniment of grand music finishing, perhaps, with a final song*

FURNITURE AND PROPERTY LIST

NOTE: The following list only includes articles of furniture and properties referred to in the text. Please see the Author's Note on page v.

ACT I
SCENE 1

On stage: Tree cut-out. *On it:* placard which reads: "A Wood"

SCENE 2

On stage: Interior cottage cut-out with window and practical door
Hearth. *In it:* vat containing ragged, torn pair of combinations. *By it:* bottle of lye
Table
3 chairs

Off stage: Feathers **(Hortense)**

Personal: **Edward:** coins in pocket

SCENE 3

On stage: Tree cut-out as before

Personal: **Xenia:** rope round neck, initialled handkerchief in hand

SCENE 4

On stage: Interior cottage cut-out as before
Hearth. *In it:* vat
Table
3 chairs

Off stage: Initialled handkerchief **(Bela)**

Personal: **Bela:** 2 silver charm necklaces

ACT II
SCENE 1

On stage: Free standing lattice window
Table
Armchair

Off stage: Placard which reads: "Act II, nine months later" **(stage management)**

The Gypsy's Revenge   39

                                    SCENE 2
On stage: Tree cut-out as before

Off stage: Silver-headed walking stick, lantern **(Edward)**

Personal: **Bela:** bottle

On stage: Interior cottage cut-out as before
              Hearth. *In it:* vat. *By it:* bucket
              Table. *On it:* dead rabbit (for **Hortense**)
              3 chairs
              Crate with piece of blanket. *In crate:* rabbit skin

Off stage: Cup of milk **(Hortense)**

                                    SCENE 4
On stage: Tree cut-out as before

Off stage: Large bottle marked with skull and crossbones **(Bela)**

Personal: **Edward:** coins in pocket

                                    SCENE 5
On stage: Interior cottage cut-out as before
              Hearth. *In it:* vat
              Table
              3 chairs
              Crate

Personal: **Mr Mudd:** coins
              Edward: large bottle marked with skull and crossbones

                                    SCENE 6
On stage: Tree cut-out as before

Off stage: Shovel **(Jethro)**

                                    SCENE 7
On stage: Free standing lattice window as before
              Table. *On it:* two tumblers of drink **(Mabel)**
              Dagger **(Mr Mudd)**

                                    ACT III
                                    SCENE 1
On stage: Interior cottage cut-out as before
              Hearth. *In it:* vat
              Table
              3 chairs

Personal: **Hortense:** silver charm necklace
Victoria: silver charm necklace
Jethro: enormous ring

Scene 2

On stage: Free standing lattice window as before
Table
Armchair
Glass (for **Edward**)

Scene 3

On stage: Tree cut-out as before
Grave. *By it:* mound of earth, spade (for **Edward**)

Personal: **Victoria:** silver charm necklace

Scene 4

On stage: Interior cottage cut-out as before
Hearth. *In it:* vat. *By it:* hammer
Table
3 chairs

Personal: **Hortense:** silver charm necklace

Scene 5

On stage: Tree cut-out as before

Off stage: Lantern **(Jethro)**

Personal: **Hortense:** gun

LIGHTING PLOT

The following plot indicates cues necessary to the action. Additions such as green spots for Edward, etc., may be made if facilities permit. Please see the Author's Note on page v.

Property fittings required: nil
Various simple settings on an open stage

ACT I

To open: Fading exterior winter light

Cue 1	After **Bela** and **Xenia** enter *Night deepens*	(Page 3)
Cue 2	**Bela:** "But see—the moon!" *Slowly bring up full moonlight effect*	(Page 3)
Cue 3	At the end of SCENE 1 *Crossfade to interior cottage lighting*	(Page 5)
Cue 4	At the end of SCENE 2 *Crossfade to exterior night effect*	(Page 8)
Cue 5	**Bela:** "... they shall confirm my darkest doubts." *Bring up moonlight effect*	(Page 9)
Cue 6	**Bela** howls piteously *Fade to Black-out*	(Page 9)
Cue 7	To open SCENE 4 *Bring up interior cottage lighting*	(Page 9)

ACT II

To open: Overall interior lighting

Cue 8	At the end of SCENE 1 *Crossfade to exterior night effect*	(Page 16)
Cue 9	**Bela** and **Edward** grapple *Lightning*	(Page 17)
Cue 10	**Edward:** "And now for the mother!" *Dim lighting and bring up "luminous eyes" effect*	(Page 17)
Cue 11	**Edward** exits, flailing *Slowly bring up dawn effect*	(Page 17)
Cue 12	To open SCENE 3 *Bring up overall interior lighting*	(Page 17)
Cue 13	At the end of SCENE 3 *Crossfade to exterior daylight effect*	(Page 20)

Cue 14	At the end of SCENE 4 Crossfade to overall interior lighting	(Page 22)
Cue 15	At the end of SCENE 5 Crossfade to exterior daylight effect	(Page 24)
Cue 16	**Bela:** "... guide your father to his just revenge!" Change to red sunset effect sharply silhouetting **Bela**	(Page 27)
Cue 17	To open SCENE 7 Bring up gloomy interior lighting with fitful moonlight effect through window	(Page 27)
Cue 18	**Edward:** "Die! Die! You whore!" Lightning	(Page 28)
Cue 19	**Mr Mudd** appears at the window Lightning	(Page 28)
Cue 20	**Bela:** "Doomed to eternal damnation!" Lightning	(Page 29)

ACT III

To open: Overall interior lighting

Cue 21	At the end of SCENE 1 Crossfade to gloomy interior lighting	(Page 31)
Cue 22	**Edward:** "Forgive me, Lord." Lightning	(Page 33)
Cue 23	**Edward:** "I put my faith in hell." Lightning	(Page 33)
Cue 24	**Edward:** "Now, God, do your worst!" Lightning	(Page 33)
Cue 25	**Edward** starts to drag the body off Lightning	(Page 33)
Cue 26	At the end of SCENE 2 Crossfade to exterior full moonlight effect	(Page 33)
Cue 27	**Edward:** "I shall fetch her." Black-out, then return to previous lighting	(Page 34)
Cue 28	**Edward:** "... who already lingers here!" Lightning	(Page 34)
Cue 29	To open SCENE 4 Bring up gloomy interior lighting with lightning effect	(Page 35)
Cue 30	At the end of SCENE 4 Crossfade to exterior night effect	(Page 35)
Cue 31	When the CURTAIN rises on the whole company Bring up full general lighting	(Page 37)

EFFECTS PLOT

ACT I

Cue 1	**Edward:** "... nor the powers of darkness." *Owl hoot and animal scream*	(Page 2)
Cue 2	**Xenia:** "... to protect my poor father." *Distant howl*	(Page 3)
Cue 3	**Jethro:** "... in this dratted wood, in the dark." *Howl*	(Page 4)
Cue 4	**Jethro:** "... nowhere to spend the night alone." *Owl hoot*	(Page 4)
Cue 5	After **Jethro** exits, leading the werewolf by the hand *Ferocious snarling and screaming*	(Page 4)
Cue 6	**Jethro** (*off*): "... you naughty flibber-me-gibbet." *Shriek and howl*	(Page 4)
Cue 7	As SCENE 2 opens *Pig squealing*	(Page 5)
Cue 8	**Bela:** "As will the curse of the werewolf!" *Thunder*	(Page 8)
Cue 9	As SCENE 3 opens *Howling noises and owl hooting*	(Page 9)

ACT II

Cue 10	**Bela:** "... the children of the night to protect you." *Howling noises*	(Page 16)
Cue 11	**Bela:** "... as if they be your own!" *Howling and hooting noises*	(Page 16)
Cue 12	**Bela:** "... the child of Satan!" *Thunder and howling noises*	(Page 17)
Cue 13	**Edward:** "And now for the mother!" *Hideous howling, grunting and flapping noises*	(Page 17)
Cue 14	After **Edward** exits, flailing *Bird singing and baby cries*	(Page 17)
Cue 15	**Mr Mudd:** "Here, baby, play with this!" *Chomping sounds followed by a belch*	(Page 20)
Cue 16	**Hortense** exits *Baby cries*	(Page 20)
Cue 17	To open SCENE 7 *Howling and thunder*	(Page 27)

Cue 18	**Mabel:** "Must think I'm daft." *Howling and thunder*	(Page 27)
Cue 19	**Edward:** "Die! Die! You whore!" *Thunder*	(Page 28)
Cue 20	**Edward:** "Now, how to dispose of the body?" *Loud howl*	(Page 28)
Cue 21	**Mr Mudd** appears at the window *Thunder*	(Page 28)
Cue 22	**Bela:** "Doomed to eternal damnation!" *Loud thunder*	(Page 29)

ACT III

Cue 23	To open SCENE 2 *Thunder*	(Page 31)
Cue 24	**Edward:** "... as the clock strikes eight." *Clock chimes seven*	(Page 31)
Cue 25	**Edward:** "Only seven o'clock. Thank God." *Clock chime*	(Page 31)
Cue 26	**Ghosts** (*wailing together*): "Farewell!" *Thunder*	(Page 32)
Cue 27	**Edward:** "What rubbish!" *Knock at door*	(Page 32)
Cue 28	**Edward:** "Forgive me, Lord." *Crash of thunder*	(Page 33)
Cue 29	**Edward:** "I put my faith in hell." *Thunder*	(Page 33)
Cue 30	**Edward:** "Now, God, do your worst!" *Thunder*	(Page 33)
Cue 31	**Edward:** "... your final place of rest!" *Thunder*	(Page 33)
Cue 32	**Edward:** "... who already lingers here!" *Thunder*	(Page 34)
Cue 33	To open SCENE 4 *Thunder*	(Page 35)
Cue 34	To open SCENE 5 *Thunder*	(Page 36)
Cue 35	**Jethro** fires the gun *Gun shot*	(Page 36)